The World Behind the World

Also by April Bernard

POETRY

Brawl & Jag
Romanticism
Swan Electric
Psalms
Blackbird Bye Bye

NOVELS

Pirate Jenny
Miss Fuller

The World
Behind the World

Poems

April Bernard

W. W. NORTON & COMPANY
Celebrating a Century of Independent Publishing

For information about permission to reproduce selections from this book,
write to Permissions, W. W. Norton & Company, Inc.,
500 Fifth Avenue, New York, NY 10110

For information about special discounts for bulk purchases,
please contact W. W. Norton Special Sales at
specialsales@wwnorton.com or 800-233-4830

Manufacturing by Versa Press
Production manager: Louise Mattarelliano

ISBN 978-1-324-03620-3

W. W. Norton & Company, Inc., 500 Fifth Avenue, New York, N.Y. 10110
www.wwnorton.com

W. W. Norton & Company Ltd., 15 Carlisle Street, London W1D 3BS

1 2 3 4 5 6 7 8 9 0

Contents

3.

1.

Haunt

Six months after death, my mother
has come to haunt me. Ever
the opportunist, she finds the virus
lockdown a handy time to slide
into the slot for my shadow, as if
I faced the sun at an angle of forty-
five degrees. There she is, darkening
my starboard periphery un-
smiling, reaching cold mist hands
into mine to whisk the eggs, fold
the sheets, sort the papers, choose
spools of thread for stitching
another face mask. This is her kind
of catastrophe, rife with irony and fear
and small domestic refinements
of infinite unimportance as we sail
about the house and yard, posing
for no one. I once thought
ghosts made "appearances," but she
eludes sight: dodgy, palpable,
squeezing in for one last clutch
at the stuff of my survival.

"Lord, crack their teeth"

from Mary Sidney's Psalms

now-met the smart-mouths
who say *get on the train*
it's leaving the station mocking

my age my suddenly
indefensible life's work's
allegiance to words; trickery

turns to make me out
a villainess in a polar-bear coat
who's *too articulate* drenched

in melting polar-ice stranded
and drenched; was every new
generation so cruel o lord or lady

of the skies who rules
alike the stippling strati and
thunderheads send your bolts

to crack their idiot teeth smack
their smiles; I weary of
placation; to dust lord them grind

Seal

I met a big-headed seal, once, in cold water where Nantucket
Island falls off fast into deep currents by Sankaty Light. For a long
while we swam, never nearer than my arm's length, but together. It
seemed he could tread water while remaining completely still, just
his whiskers quivering with effort and his face, eyes droopy but
mouth curled up, like he was about to laugh. When I called *Hello,
hello there*, he came close but never let me touch his shiny dappled
grey-and-tawny fur. The seal made me so happy that water and
air became one medium as we inhabited that other world, where
nothing human can wreck us. It smells of salt and iodine, and it
holds us as we were meant to be held, cold but stirring ourselves
to heat; perfect. For how long? It was I who ended it, winded and
afraid, almost too late to make it back to shore. Deplore with
me: all the pain our clever brains, self-winding like watches that
won't stop, make in the world, so that we spend half our waking
lives taking medicine to stop it. I would give anything to be back
there now, in that water. From the steep beach I watched the seal
watching me for a long time as the light of late summer left us,
streaking in harsh shadows that purpled the sea. He was still
there, watching, inviting, until I turned my back to climb the dune.

The world has split

into a farce that plays
on two landings of the same
staircase. Yes: Treachery

gnaws the planks
of the state, so as
to tip us off, and out.

Allen v Farrow

We don't know
what we want or who we are
we don't even agree we are we
In a civilized society, you say,
preface to: we do not hurt
children, we do not fuck children,
we define childhood,
of course we say we do, and
we know we mean *we* as in,
we adults who agree to follow rules
Almost no adult I know
follows all rules; look at that one
make an exception as she takes
a handicap space, or he makes
an exception for tax deductions,
or sorting his recyclables, or
fucking children
There must be rules
we say, but in some place,
in some other country, a father
sells his daughter, at 14,
and she has her menses
so she is not by definition a child
Throw your hands into the air
and say, *in a civilized society,*
this could not happen
but she is 14, she is a woman,
and respecting tradition,

even foul tradition, what
do you mean by civilized,
of course she is for sale
and will be fucked and that
may well be the least of it
14? 19? 8? sold? lured?
Look at this country, now,
look at him, and him, and him
Doesn't money grant
the power to define civilized,
isn't that what it's for,
to make anything plausible

"My louring head so low"

from a poem by George Gascoigne

The usual trajectory:
Dejection swathes the head in clouds,
in rain; some tolling bells; a half-
remembered half-regretted scene
of youthful love; comes yet more rain
now icicled to spikes of sleet
that slide beneath the overcoat
to scald the skin and pull the chin
down lower, glowering, until
at last, hope sprung upon a sun-
set beam, the head lifts up from lour
in prayerful utterance of thanks
as thrush-song marks the storm's
surcease. Just not this time.

The Spell

Grizzly, flossy brown,
sticky from the berry patch:
Beware the hunter
who slips amid the bracken
and covets your pelt. Come here
into this cave I found. I will

cast a spell to render you
tame. Let me crawl inside
your overcoat, wear your head
upon my head. Heavy paws
with pads and claws
clatter floppy on my hands.

You see, I am another sort of hunter.
You see, I am not your friend.

"Wreathed with error"

from a poem by Thomas Wyatt

impossible not
to weigh the chain
of events of life
of mine of when
of where of how
every ring
of iron of blood
dropped and looped
upon the loop
below a chain
wound up
the capstan spool
to make a wreath
of grief of grind
of crunch in feather-
boa links
of iron of blood
to decorate
the vanity
the self-concern
the careless laugh
that hurt the lover
that lost the bet
that missed the step
that clutched

the wreath of ever-
green of rings
of tin of paper
chains around
a tree a spool
a waist so tight
and rusted stu-
pefied by envy
by anger by lust
impeding breath
and hands the will
to recollect
to remedy

"My thoughts are eagles' food"

from a poem by Fulke Greville

I seek aid: My grandmother's gilt
clock that plays Greensleeves
now fills me with dread; can you
muffle its sharp-tooth chime?
Dab my forehead with rose water,
sing me a song I never heard before,
tell me something to make me laugh
and rest content—a state unknown.
My thoughts run races, mousey
and fearful, scattering to the edges
of the autumn lawn. Leave them
to the raptors, now. Shame
turns out to be a choice, a wire taut
on the trap we set ourselves, of use until it's not.

Who Falters

after the Tang poets

Where now is the laughter
that lit and shook my house
like rain sliding off
the leaves after a storm?
Who falters as she lifts her hand?
Where, for that matter, is the sun?
This much is certain:
Nameless I have become,
and without kin.
I fought my battles
under the emperor's pennant;
then I fought my friends,
all of them, until
they left me too.
The capital city where I thrived
survives in name only;
crazy rich people
have colonized it like sea-
birds covering a rocky isthmus
with white slick streaks
and incalculable din.
I grasp my own hand,
so that for once
I might touch flesh.
Did you hear—?
that sharp knock—at the door.

Self-Portrait as a Shaker Dwelling

unbent
unsmiling
half-harvested
not tangled
squared off
deloused
unengulphed
not unhouseled
not knotty
not weeping
lavenderish
post-prelapsarian
shut
noiseless
staked
yarrow-dyed
defathered
planed
knit-up
hinged
dovetailed
unshook
unshocked
not simple
not free

The Fetch Explained, More or Less

A *fetch*, that folklore spirit, cannot be
a dog. My dog *fetches*, though
we do not use that command. *Fetch,*
a new adjective—"that's so fetch"—
from the former *fetching*, also
an adjective, gerund of the verb,
suggests something so dear
as to have fetched us away
from ourselves, from our first
resistance. Note that the fetch, noun,
will not oblige: She's catlike, but not fluff,
not available for petting; nor warm, nor hissing.
A fetch is not a *familiar*.

                    A familiar may
be a cat, mewing slinky about the feet,
or crow or parrot or helplessly gesturing
raccoon enlisted to assist in casting
spells and brewing the specific potion to make
an enemy's privates rot. Miniature dogs
in fashion totes are not familiars, howsoever
witchy their porters, long of limb and fixed
of purpose.

                    My dog Buster, ginger and foxy,
is not familiar not fetch not *spirit-animal*;
he is, rather, my attendant, dependent, lode-star,
pest, sentinel-Magog, house-angel, noise-maker,

secretary, nurse-maid, critic. His alternate names:
Bingo Little, Little Mister, Little B, Little
Bun, Honey Bun. You must draw your own
conclusions.

       The fetch is self's companion self,
visiting from the world behind the world,
the female spirit of Norse lore also called
a *Fylgja*. I am pleased to learn her proper name
at last. In my childhood bedroom she
required her own pillow, blue-striped percale,
for sleepovers, and always woke me with a shake.
Some say the fetch is animal (no), or signals
coming death (no, as mine has hung around
off and on all the years I have survived).
On arrival, my fetch lights a match to the crown-
wick of my head, firing up not soul but
will. With her I have been Dionyzia in *Pericles,*
lived Hamlet, Cymbeline, and Hedda Gabler,
have climbed a water tower while almost dead
of fright, danced the real tango in a taverna,
swum on summer nights for hours beneath
an orange psilocybin-cap moon. I have
written and painted and birthed and swooned
as she urged me on.

       My oldest friend,
she knows me well enough to sit for hours

in these later days, drinking tea while
reviewing time and chance. Sometimes
she lashed out, perilously, when will
zagged into impulse, and we recall
our close calls: The wrecked car, the sunk
boat, assorted acts in 3 a.m. corners,
the screenplays, eight whole years
in thrall to an aesthete thug. Also:
an audition for tv book-chat host,
the shotgun, the sneak-thief,
delirium on a footbridge, a pink wig,
such love as I was given, and squandered. . . .
And *jodhpurs*, of all things, and lies I sold
and lies I bought, every shame and slipup
dangling like wind-chime folk-art trash-bits
from a dead tree in the front yard.
                                         Fylgja,
fetch me memories good and bad,
retrieve those tossed-away times. Now
after all she is a death-watch, since
every lived moment is another one closer
to death, and yet she hastens me on to more life,

breathing faster as days shorten. Hot-headed,
laughing, we giddy suffering creatures
barely keep pace with our fetches, who fare
into darkness before us, sharpening their teeth.

2.

Cold Morning

A horse lay on the ground, ringed
by sentinel horses of the same dark brown

like a monochrome drawing, only not a drawing,
early morning, a cold morning, beside the county road.

I walked the drainage ditch to the fence
and as no animal moved I became certain of death.

The horses bowed their heads to sniff
the dead one. Frost rimed the mud, dully, lit

by the dull low sun. Seven years ago my friend
died and I am still outraged. I have been

shaking my stupid fist of outrage at the gods
for so long they must have a nickname for me,

like Dryope, for the black poplar tree,
or else Sophia, as a joke, since

I have no wisdom. Only petty malevolence
could have dreamed up three kinds of cancer

to rot away one of earth's best creatures—
noble *as a horse*, keen *as an eagle*, tender

as a good mother, the only man whose hand
I held without fear or need. Later, on the car radio,

a strange bulletin: Escaped bison swam the Hudson,
blundered onto the Interstate, and then were killed

by marksmen. Fifteen of them, also dark
brown, like my friend, whose hair and brows were dark,

the dark manes of the animals dead, and gathering.

"My care is like my shadow"

from a poem by Elizabeth I of England

Trailing, moored to my ankle
and bent to the sun's angle:
my great care. I was orphaned the day
I was born; my mother turned away
alive but with no filament to bind me.
She clutches still but cannot find me,
she's heavy empty, my care her name.
And still I halt and fill with shame
she did not care for me, did not bind
me together. That lack unwinds
still, my care her name my shadow trips
me and won't let go unless I slip
into that night, unbounded sweet,
knit sunless up, that flies to meet
me: careless, un-shadowed, foot-fleet.

"Such hap as I am happed in"

from a poem by Thomas Wyatt

In each photo, bunchy heavy
rugs and wraps fail to disguise,
instead delineate seated "invisible"
mothers beneath. Capturing such hap
as we all get happed in, studio
daguerreotypes froze children held
and propped by draped figures
molded as lumpy laps so that
history may prize these prizes,
though mostly it will not. Fretful
or slumped or wisely patient,
each copper-plate child augurs
familiar nineteenth-century agonies.
We ponder rickets, battlefields,
consumption, boredom, syphilis,
a horse's kick upside the head.
See this one, perhaps a boy, up-
lift a fist with one finger crooked.
He's like an infant Jesus altar-piece,
but for the twisted lip that sneers:
"Look for the world behind the world,
if you like, but—." Allowing
no inroad to the spirit, nor hope
for the one who bore and bears him, he
awaits such days as will hurtle him,
barreling, to his happenstance.

"The root uprear'd shall be"

from a poem by Elizabeth I of England

Fingerlings that clawed the earth
and made of life a living death
in cataclysmic rainstorm jolt
and yank and, losing, loose their hold.
A crack: the parent fir-trees fall,
exposing root-fringe, dripping shawl.
Below, an opened cavern curls
into the singing underworld:
a beetle's buzzing purple back,
a chipmunk's whistle, and one black
eye in a hissing toothy face
that quickly disappears. A trace
of silver green, the lichen's pocked
fan, spreads across granitic rock;
bark sags from trunks, ribbands
loosened off the roll. The woodland
where these spires stood for centuries
now loses certainty; as drizzly
monuments dissolve, each dint
and dimple, in fainting print
upon the path, wells up and smears.
Monarchs, firs, and saints are cleared
from childhood's familiar copse.
It's time to saw and split and lop
the branches. Ah—! Sunlight spills a jet
of gold. This waste's a richness, yet.

Closest is music

; we hear God there.
All shared harmonies
tune it into being:
dance, pipes, a room
of students reading the long
poem by Ashbery aloud.
It's there as well in Brian
Wilson singing *God*
only knows. The atheists
still insisting must not
be able to hear those
harmonies shake God
or *something else* to life,
and I pity them, as I
pitied my father, dying
as his unbelief wavered—
("not God, but *some*
thing else," he said)—
almost hearing the shimmer
strings of Monsalvat.
Making music we
make God thereby,
or a simulacrum
so powerful I fear
to meet the real thing.
But: Hopkins promises
through the features of men's
faces we may discover

it: my father's chin-up
profile stark as an Indian-
head nickel. Already
knowing loved faces,
says the priest,
when we meet God's
we will at last be able
to slide heaven-notes
along our throats, timbrels
shaking in no fear.

The Legacy of Nicholas Ray

We were shiny new and
you can't imagine how pretty.
He wore a Swedish police
motorcycle jacket and still
had his sleek blond hair but we
didn't say "still has"; we did
not see. I wore rayon blouses
from the thrift store, figured
with strawberries and bluebirds
or green-and-yellow parallelograms
and black rayon split skirts. His
chunk-black boots; my
nile-green sling-backs. I still had
my figure. We were just a little
too pretty for a Nicholas Ray
picture, we loved those pictures,
but did not see how broken
we already were under our shiny
shells, broken as Ida or Humphrey
or Robert Ryan. I see those movies
now, see Robert Ryan's baffled face
slowly cracking into meanness
and grief. Now I say: "Hiya, Bob,

I could be looking in the mirror."
I say: "Hey Gloria, twist your lipstick
round that cigarette. Don't I
see it all clear."

Swishing Tails of Horses, October

Mine, says the glorious yearling claiming
the path, a rubber runner laid to save her feet.

She will be bought by a Saudi prince and stabled
in Australia, though she does not, cannot, know

her exact luck, this rosy grey Miss Universe
with mischief in her dark eye, the one eye

I can see as she prances her marketed flesh past
my porch. It may be in time that she will race;

or failing that, will be allowed to breed, or live, or
not. I live by the auction house; I know

the scents and rhythms of the trade by now. How
mistaken she is, believing she owns anything.

Blue Jay Blues

Woke up this morning
The sun was going down
Woke up this morning
The sun was going down
Seems there used to be a sun
Busy rising when I needed one around

Woke up this morning
Grey cat in my bed
Woke up this morning
Wallace Stevens in my bed
I spent the whole day stumbling
Bees and honey filling up my head

Blue Jay came
To Mockingbird Hill
Blue Jay and me
Lived on Mockingbird Hill
When Blue Jay flew away
He left a blue feather on the windowsill

When I lay down at night
Everything goes wrong
When I lay down tonight
You'll still be dead and gone
There's a long time left to live
And so much to be done

Get me a motorcycle
And I'll ride right out of here
Get me my hearse-black motorcycle
And I'll tear right out of here
Crying so hard the wind
Makes a hurricane out of tears

Woke up this morning
Everything the same
Woke up this morning
Same name, same hands and feet
I promise when I get around to changing
You will still recognize me when we meet

Cloud Ekphrastics

Mash-Up: Italian Fresco + Mughal Fresco

Tiepolo rock-candy mountains and flossy
sugar-spun clouds bubble beneath cherubim
delineating a cosmos we can bear to inhabit. Or
visit the Jodhpur Palace, where elephants
carry armored monkeys into battle, while
at the eastern edge of the panorama other monkeys
swim away in the thick-limned tresses of a golden stream.
Above, more clouds: black and gold and curled into paisley,
swirling into the fresco, a multiple heaven
of stories and salvation, suitable for bedtime.

Shaker Village Brick Dwelling

Demented lollipop
spirit-drawings made
by Mother Ann's
timid creatures,
bushes and trees with tidy
symmetrical spokes
shrieking from the dreams
of wool-and-pine-board
bed-shackled bodies
denied the wet curl
of erotic relief: Only
stern children, chastened,

build houses straight
as these, where hoods
and swathes of dead thistle
hang dry as wrung-out clouds
on prim pegs.

Child's Drawing

Behold a figure chalked on thick grey paper,
perhaps a snowman: He moves
lopsided as a pet ghost or a grounded cloud
into blue snow, and owns his own blue distance.

This Life

I would be the dove, tucked
in the heavy arbor, listening to rain
tap the leaf lobes. I would be the bear,
stupid beneath the snow.

Say a syringe came to tease me with relief,
offering my stretch of earth: for this,
I would pay even the jewels of poetry.
But bribes don't work.

Did I agree to this? The sages tell us
that blindness in the morning
may give way to sight by evening. . . .

How they lie. We know only a little more
than the animals, and it is pain. This life
that demands, with every sun-up, to be lived.

Proleptic

Caved, hanging batlike since time woke,
she predicted Pangea's cleaving, the Middle
Passage, the burnt Armada, even
my mother's gastric volvulus—
the flipped-over stomach, pinched
at both ends, that killed her. The seer's
visions mage the world. Yahweh,
the Kami, Shiva, men ranting and women
scrying teacup sludge, all make her laugh.
Getting it wrong is half our fate; every
outcome that could have been heads
but was tails made luck for someone
else. She invented *zero-sum*, the nightly
sweep of bony wing over the table
to send the anagram tiles flying,
adding *less* to *hope* as *light* twists
into *ligature*, *giver* crumbles into *grave*.

3.

Not another dead deer

poem, please. Your Grandpa
Cappy "passed away"
invisibly, and that neighbor
with the eyepatch who flipped
it up at a cocktail party
never got invited back. So
for you a deer carcass,
in all its plaintive moods, signals
the death of beauty, innocence,
nature itself.
         There's a road
I travel around and back
like a maze-rat in upstate
New York, where people
drive too fast. In early spring I
call it Shiloh, for its battlefield
litter of raccoons and rictus-
grinning possums, half-
foxes, dogs, cats, and deer
with barrel-butts slumped
into gravel and tawny breasts
blackened, caved in, eyes
pecked out by buzzards—
but it eludes allegory,

this Shiloh. The war waged
by our cars on their bodies
is disgusting but moot.
Write about something else.

You can sing it

—I tell students, that Hopkins poem,
to the tune of the Doxology,
"old one hundredth" in the hymn book.
In the choir at St. Raphael's,
"Praise God from whom all bles-sings
flow" flowed in our treble tremble
all the way to "Praise Fa-ther, Son,
and Ho-ly Ghost. A-men." We sang
it swooped from the rafters,
breathing down over the backs
of the churchgoers, in thrall
to Dr. Dumain. Unwilling to be
mediocre, he rehearsed us
several nights a week, a scraggle
of twelve girls coaxed and bullied
into making real music. His hands
and feet paddled at the organ
as he conducted with jutted
chin and wild brows. Almost too
pure was our "Re-joice, Re-
joice, E-ma-a-an-u-el," all the dusky
days of Advent. When, years later,
I wandered alone into the Matisse
Chapel in Provence, I sang those
hymns to hear an ice-water tone
the chalk cave gave.

And now,
reading Hopkins, puzzling out
his odd-ball meters, I hear how
the poet heard his sprung feet
as measures of music, with
the strong accent a long "whole"
note, assorted less-heavy beats
a cherubic array of fleeting fourths
and eighths. Here's "Pied
Beauty," which begins "Glo-ry
be to God for dap-pled things,"
another Doxology, and drops
the after-thought "Praise him," an
"A-men." You have to speed the tongue
through "What-ev-er is fick-le, freck-led
(who knows how?) / With swift, slow; sweet
sour; a-daz-zle, dim. . . ."
                                    I tell students,
you can sing it, and we do; his words
match exactly that old hundredth, lilting
creation's errors and accidents
to mottle a vista that leads,
in variable measures, to the world

behind the world, where raggedy
becomes pattern and a staggered
amen in dappling laps whole.

"This wound shall heal again"

from a poem by Thomas Wyatt

Eleven years we talked, chairs
canted; sometimes we looked

at one another, or as easily turned
to gaze through plate-glass

into the trees at the birds
who came in all seasons

to the feeders, in quick dips
and pauses of flight so like

our speech. How amused
he was I knew their names—junco,

grosbeak, jay—names he never
looked up, or cared to learn.

A useful father and mother
in one creature: this home-made

chimera taught me, hour by hour.
I knew him completely but now

that he is dead, not at all.
I conjure the better version

of self he offered, which I wrote
on my brain for reference,

trust in him expanding
to trust in myself. That

is how it is supposed to work,
the much-mocked talk-talk

for healing wounds both rare
and common. If only

his big knob head could turn
to me again, bland and serene

as a cow's in the pasture turning
to the sun for warmth. He said

he cherished my warmth, that
he trusted me: to raise my son,

do my work, be kind, fare
forward—all that, all that.

Tree-crazy

like this maple, beckoning
with finger-twigs, laughter
cascading down its greeny arms,
about to shake loose into *enargeia*,
the god's arrival not as other

but as "bright unbearable reality"

as two herons shoulder up
from the pond, conferring, probably,
about minnows before one wing
flies out, drawing a blade
to open the sky's throat, sun-struck

they are birds no longer

so, shuddering, I ask that I might
be let into this brightness, even
though it meant the end of me
as I might now cohere, while
tiers of maple leaves tumble forward,

eager to shred me into light

Sora, I see you

in this ink drawing,
bundled in quilted cotton
for the cold, leading a pony
on which the master, Bashō,
sits. Your footwear: socks
with sandals, wooden *geta*
improbable for hiking,
let alone wading through snow.
How cheerfully, like all
sidekicks, you offer
as needed straight lines
or ripostes; and with
what kindness the master
adds your verse to his.
Purple clover pokes through dry grass
the children trample
with happy cries.
It's plain you want
to clown even more
than admire the moon,
and that your poems
stick out at the elbows.
Bashō is the genius:
This road without travelers
leads only

to autumn's end.
You are worn thin, a servant-
shadow, yet you do not
complain. Sturdy you bear him
on his last road, as
archivist, almost as widow.

Why

I was 24, he barely older but seemed
ancient as a glamour changeling,

an alien dropped into the city who knew
it all, and since everyone loved him,

I was no exception—besotted like you
when your second cousin careened into

the driveway in a muscle car and
taught you how to drink bourbon

with beer back, like that—only
his secrets were Kafka, and Burroughs,

Colette, Artaud, Jack Smith, and a first-name
acquaintance with the Bowery Boys

because all history is in the present tense.
In his hands, I became

another trove of detail: he itemized
French lips and clever words,

yellow rain boots, brave soprano,
a knack for fixing broken things,

and put me in his pantheon. A coterie
of appreciation tracked his distinctive

gait; bouncing on his toes like a curator
of the world anxious not to mar

what he explores, he loped
the streets of the city wolfishly surveying,

pausing to roll another Gauloise. Film-
makers and painters and musicians

sought the perfect pitch of his advice, he
meanwhile tormented by inanition

as if in Poe's collapsing iron room of fire—
and yet when it was all too much,

had almost gone too far, he could *produce*—
enough words to defy the demons,

proving again he was *all of that*.
Everyone wanted to protect

him, protecting what one idolizes
a necessary feature of worship,

though they did not guess
what he thought of them, or said

he did. Rage and envy unhinged
his deep late hours.—But still

I wish I could make you hear
his wry daytime reads on

the world, the deep laconic voice
of an old-timey movie star,

its own clarion *No*
becoming, with time, a version of

Yes, laughing darkly. Whatever
delusions he was prey to

he made half-real, at least. Perhaps
after all, "nutrition" *is* a scam; perhaps

the mummy in the tomb is still
alive after three thousand years, all

photographs are deliberate lies, and
the desire to fuck a leg wound, like in

J. G. Ballard's *Crash*, has useful meaning.
Maybe it does. Such things

sometimes still seem plausible. Not yet
fully mad, in his un-wounded skin,

he smelled like the dusky pine needles and
woodstove smoke of my childhood

by the lake—home, only more so.

Fish Life

A fishercat
tugged claws
through my gills
hung me gaffed
shining and flinging
myself to silver shards
spinning and gasping
until I wrenched
away

down
into the deep
opening laving
loosely as I turned
in the pine-ringed lake
ice warmed to velvet
turning again to
pass deeper
down

Like Jonah

1. *"he layed him down and slombred"*

   from the Book of Jonah, Coverdale translation

Sleep-stumbling: half a day or so cranked to apparent
functionality, like an appliance past its warranty, suddenly

making *that noise* and just grinding down. So when God
orders a mission, say: The heck with that; regular life is hard

enough, now I should save Nineveh? Instead Jonah stows away below
decks in the first grubby tar-caulked ship he finds. Lays down

his weary body in slombre. While hail buck-shots, he kitten-
curls to take an unearned nap, content to bring the world to wreck.

2. *"in the belly of the fysh"*

Sailors find him, curse of their voyage, and must toss
him to the storm. Well, that shakes him up. Salt

flows into every hole, through pores; he's scarcely
a body at all, more like a bread crust dissolving into broth,

just as the great fysh swallows him up. Shark, whale, giant squid,
whatever leviathan, it's got him now. It turns out its gut

is surprisingly like a motel room, if you are hungover and someone
has stolen your wallet and car. The linens itch. He never

wanted to think. But the ribbed ceiling and stench declare:
It's a fysh-belly Hi-Way Inn and God has stuck you here. Think.

3. *"thre dayes and thre nightes"*

What I've been thinking, from a Hindu scholar:
"Let come what comes, let go what goes. Study what remains."

I like "study," the word suggesting what life has
taught me already, that almost nothing is so terrible it cannot

also be of interest. But that's not how Jehovah, the God
of our fathers, works. So if the dark stink in the mouth of my self-

swallowed soul can ever let me out, I must think
on other things. Like Jonah, let me sit on this pile of fysh bones

and try. In my version, an angel arrives to condole with me
about the gas that slinks the halls where we teach, sliming

up beauty, befouling what we hold dear. It's not as if I expected
art to *thrive*. But time's tide has jacked backwards;

we wander the Pentateuchal plains, righteous wrath
chasing us; they've already stoned the angels and subangels foolish

enough to speak in verse. We retreat into dull mutters,
eyes averted, but still they call us Jezebel, predict our bodies

eaten by dogs at the gates of Jezreel, or Nineveh, or Sodom.
Oh, for some new power! Oh, to be—even—Jonah!

Say now what once I wanted from men: A ready,
laughing muscle, a forwardness, I wanted them to push

that power into me, so I'd move easy through the world
grinning and throwing an uppercut, or a flash

haymaker—until at last I gave up that desire, as if
relinquishment, a nunnish renunciation, would be

a kind of victory. Only it is not. It certainly is not.
See what powerlessness has wrought, and see it's time

to change my mind again. Not someone else's step and fist,
but my own, is now I fear required. Doubtful I fret.

4. *"for why?"*

Like Jonah, wide awake, I am vomited out on dry land.

Intercessionary: 2021

October noon darkens
too early, every day rain

this year: cold wet summer
and cold wet after-summer,

with no turn of leaves
to turn a heart.

A spectral poet once
began each writing season

just about now,
as everything went dim—

she waited on daylight
savings, not saving

but spending in shadow,
flash ducat by ducat,

in a velvet-festooned attic.
Some people are just

more alive than others,
more off-the-kilter,

just *more*—

O witchy bitch,
spell me how

to write from darkness,
cut in so deep and shiny.

Woo-woo

I know it's crap, but every good person
I've ever known believes, or wants
to, in astrology, seers, psychics,
ouija boards, witches, or at the very least
Christ our Savior. To have a good
heart means the world hurts you again
and again, so you go looking for guidance,
explanations, shreds of courage,
the ghosts of those you loved, and

dive into all this woo-woo, these
"rising-sign charts," this lapis pendant to
"calm the Shen" (give me that), the voice
you heard beamed from an alternate
astral plane, coming up the stairs, in
articulated directive: "Do not take
that last step," and you do not and so
avoid the busted riser, the hole through
which you could have tumbled to a
shattered tibia and then some. Your

saintly guide is a linen-clad dervish
spinning towards you like a top, hands
folded across his chest. He has been spun
from the glowing neurons of brain net
but is no less real, no less likely to offer

respite and release from news that arrives
from all quarters. He is a vehicle for time
travel, out of time itself. Spin with him, now,
spin with him until you are humming
on your own still axis. Hum. Spin.

"Use me quiet"

from a poem by Thomas Wyatt

In slip around the corner
my cells whisper what

my son left behind;
his dna took up residence

in organs various, brain
and heart and liver;

my lights, that is, are riddled
with his bits

in mechanism unreciprocal.

Everyone said motherhood
will change you but not that

my viscera would use me
quiet by electric pulse as

pilgrims who colonize
the wilderness of my body

steadfast cry
for home, only calm

when he is near, and calm.

"Sithens in a net"

from a poem by Thomas Wyatt

What we try to snag and hold fast
of laughter, wood smoke, but especially
the necessary ignorance

to go forward, to trust: I have netted
baubles from air bubbles, pictures of cozy
life in books, the way hot cider

by a warm stove completes winter
and sunset was sunset because you said
"Look at that!" to someone you loved.

At a reading, John Ashbery was asked,
"But what was that *about*?" and he said,
"I guess I'm just sad about time,"

and who can be sorry he was sad, when
such fabric lengths of poems came off
the loom, in down-home-and-I-guess baroque.

Sometimes my dog turns, flops down,
and presses against me with a sigh that
fills the world with peace, making

permanent what would otherwise fly away
on the lash of a clock's tick. You have to think
about things in a different way, allow

ephemera to etch their brain-webs,
allow yourself to last as another beholds.

Notes and Acknowledgments

"'This wound shall heal again'" is dedicated to the memory of Dr. Richard Q. Ford. "Intercessionary: 2021" is dedicated to the memory of Lucie Brock-Broido. In "Tree-crazy," the definition of *enargeia* as "bright unbearable reality" is from classicist and translator Alice Oswald. My thanks to Michael Autrey for alerting me to this.

Versions of these poems previously appeared in *The New York Review of Books*, *Scoundrel Time*, *Plume*, *Bloodroot*, *The Bennington Review*, and *EcoTheo Review*. "Haunt" was also anthologized in *Together in a Sudden Strangeness: America's Poets Respond to the Pandemic*, edited by Alice Quinn (Knopf, 2021). "Self-Portrait as a Shaker Dwelling" appeared in the catalogue for the Tang Museum exhibition "Energy in All Directions," edited by Ian Berry. I am deeply grateful for the attention of these editors and readers.

My thanks to Jin Auh, at the Wylie Agency, for her stalwart support; and to Jill Bialosky, at W. W. Norton, for her continued faith in me.

Writing this book would not have been possible without the kindness and advice of Lisa Bernard, Bina Gogineni, Kate Greenspan, Alice Mattison, Michael O'Neill, Henry Robinson, and Mark Wunderlich.